The
LOW BUDGET
WONDER

Ramen, beyond the packet

by

Kimberly and Skyler Prescott

The Low Budget Wonder
Ramen, beyond the packet
ISBN: 978-0-9719670-1-4
Copyright © 2012
Kimberly and Skyler Prescott
thelowbudgetwonder.com

Published by Northwood Publishing, LLC
Email: sales@northwoodpublishing.com

Cover Photography & Design: Austin Prescott
Text Design: Lisa Simpson
www.SimpsonProductions.net

Dedication

To noodle lovers everywhere,
and to our family, who have eaten
a lot of them!

Contents

Adobo
(Caution: Strong flavor ahead!)

1	chicken Ramen noodle package (crunch up while in package)
2	cups water
⅔	cup onion, chopped
2 ½	tablespoons soy sauce
2	tablespoons apple cider vinegar
½	teaspoon black pepper
¼	teaspoon garlic powder or 1 garlic clove, minced
⅛	teaspoon ginger powder

STEP ❶ Combine the water, seasoning packet, pepper, vinegar, soy sauce, garlic, ginger powder, and onion in a small pan over medium heat. Cover with a lid and let it come to a boil.

STEP ❷ When the broth is boiling, take the lid off and add the noodles.

STEP ❸ Cook the noodles to your liking. When the noodles are done, pour into a bowl and enjoy.

Breakfast Omelet

1	Ramen noodle package (any flavor) (crunch up while in package)
2	cups water
2	eggs
1	teaspoon butter or nonstick cooking spray
	Any omelet toppings such as: tomatoes, mushrooms, hot sauce, green onions, cheese, salt, and pepper

STEP ❶ This step can be done on the stovetop or in the microwave.

Bring the water to a boil in a small pan. Add the noodles and cook them to your liking.

Put the noodles and water in a microwave safe bowl. Microwave for 3-4 minutes or until the noodles are done to your liking.

STEP ❷ When the noodles are done, drain off the water and set the noodles aside.

STEP ❸ Preheat a nonstick skillet over medium heat. Melt the butter in the pan or spray with non-stick cooking spray so the bottom of the pan is coated.

STEP ❹ In a separate bowl, beat the eggs together with the seasoning packet.

STEP ❺ When the skillet is hot, spread the noodles out to cover the bottom of the pan. Pour the eggs evenly over the noodles. Sprinkle on your chosen toppings.

STEP ❻ Cook until the eggs are cooked enough to flip with a spatula and cook the other side until the eggs are set (not runny). Remove to a plate and enjoy.

Broccoli Cheese Soup

1	chicken Ramen noodle package (crunch up while in package)
1	cup water
1	cup cold milk
1	cup frozen chopped broccoli
1	tablespoon all-purpose flour
2	slices of American cheese, torn into smaller pieces

STEP ❶ Put the water and broccoli in a small pan. Bring the water to a boil.

STEP ❷ When the water is boiling, add the noodles and seasoning packet and cook them to your liking.

STEP ❸ While the noodles are cooking, in a separate bowl stir the flour into the milk until smooth and there are no lumps.

STEP ❹ When the noodles are done, add the flour and milk mixture to the noodles and stir until the soup is hot (the longer you cook it, the thicker it will get, so cook it to your choice of consistency).

STEP ❺ Add the pieces of cheese. Stir the noodles until the cheese has melted and the sauce is smooth.

Pour the soup into a bowl and enjoy.

Burrito in a Bowl

Can be cooked entirely on stovetop or in microwave

1	beef Ramen noodle package (crunch up while in package)
2	cups water
½	tomato, diced
3	tablespoons of canned refried beans
1	tablespoon fresh cilantro leaves, chopped
1	green onion, chopped
¾	teaspoon of a taco seasoning packet

STEP ❶ This step can be done on the stovetop or in the microwave.

Bring the water to a boil in a small pan. Add the noodles and seasoning packet and cook them to your liking.

Put the noodles, water, and seasoning packet in a microwave safe bowl. Microwave for 3-4 minutes or until the noodles are done to your liking.

STEP ❷ When the noodles are done, add the beans, cilantro, green onion, and taco seasoning to the noodles and mix until the refried beans have dissolved.

Step ❸ Top with the diced tomatoes and enjoy.

Chicken and Dumplings

1   chicken Ramen noodle package (crunch up while in package)

2   cups water

½   cup of Bisquick or Jiffy Baking Mix

2   tablespoons of water

¼   teaspoon chicken bouillon or 1 extra Ramen chicken seasoning packet

STEP ❶ In a medium pan with a fitting lid, bring the 2 cups of water to a boil.

STEP ❷ While the water is heating, mix the Bisquick and 2 tablespoons of water in a bowl to make a dough firm enough to roll into small balls. You may have to add a little more Bisquick depending on the consistency of the batter. The dough will be a little sticky, but it will not stick all over your fingers.

STEP ❸ When the water is boiling, stir the seasoning packet and the chicken bouillon into the water.

STEP ❹ Form about 7-9 little balls from the dough and drop them into the boiling broth. Put the lid on the pan and reduce the heat to medium low. Let the dumplings cook for 5 minutes.

Note: If the soup starts to boil over, remove the pan from the heat and turn the heat down a little. When the boiling has calmed down, put the pan back over the heat and finish the 5 minutes.

STEP ❺ When the dumplings are done, they should be fluffy not doughy. Use a slotted spoon to move the dumplings out of the broth and into a bowl or dish.

STEP ❻ Add the noodles to the broth. With the lid off, raise the heat back up to medium heat and cook them to your liking.

Pour the noodles and broth into a bowl and top the soup with the dumplings. Enjoy.

Chicken Wing Ramen

1   chicken Ramen noodle package (crunch up while in package)

2   cups water

1   tablespoon of your favorite chicken wing sauce (or) make your own teriyaki wing sauce (recipe below)

Step ❶ This step can be done on the stovetop or in the microwave.

Bring the water to a boil in a small pan. Add the noodles and seasoning packet and cook them to your liking.

Put the noodles, seasoning packet, and water in a microwave safe bowl. Microwave for 3-4 minutes or until the noodles are cooked to your liking.

Step ❷ When the noodles are done, drain off the water and put the noodles into a bowl.

Step ❸ Pour the sauce over the noodles and toss to blend. Enjoy.

Teriyaki Wing Sauce

1   tablespoon soy sauce

1 ½   teaspoons honey

⅛   teaspoon ginger powder

| 1 | teaspoon molasses |
| ¼ | teaspoon garlic powder |

Mix all the sauce ingredients in a separate cup or small bowl and stir until the honey is dissolved. Pour this over the finished noodles.

Cream of Mushroom Ramen

1 beef Ramen noodle package (crunch up while in package)

1 cup water

1 cup cold milk

1 4-oz. can of sliced mushrooms, drained

1 tablespoon all-purpose flour

STEP ❶ Bring the water to a boil in a small pan. Add the noodles, mushrooms, and seasoning packet. Cook the noodles to your liking.

STEP ❷ While the noodles are cooking, in a separate bowl stir the flour into the milk until smooth and there are no lumps.

STEP ❸ When the noodles are done, stir in the flour and milk mixture. Stir until the soup is hot (the longer you cook it, the thicker it will get, so cook it to your choice of consistency).

Pour into a bowl and enjoy.

French Onion Soup

1   beef Ramen noodle package (crunch up while in package)

2   cups water

1   cup onion, chopped

1   tablespoon butter

1   slice of Swiss cheese

STEP ❶ Melt the butter in a small pan over medium heat. Add the onion and cook until the onion is brown and tender (stir often to cook evenly).

STEP ❷ When the onion is done, add the water and seasoning packet. Bring it to a boil.

STEP ❸ Add the noodles and cook them to your liking.

STEP ❹ Pour the soup into a bowl and lay the slice of cheese on top of the hot soup. Once the cheese is melted, stir it into the soup and enjoy.

Creamy Potato Soup

1	chicken Ramen noodle package (crunch up while in package)
2	cups water
1 ½	cups milk
1	small potato, peeled and diced
2	green onions, chopped

Stovetop directions

STEP ❶ Put the potato pieces in a small pan with 1 cup of water. Cover with a tight fitting lid and cook over medium heat for about 20 minutes or until they are tender and you can pierce them easily with a fork. Drain off the water and pour the cooked potatoes into a bowl. Set aside.

STEP ❷ In the same pan, bring the 2 cups of water to a boil. Add the noodles and cook them to your liking.

STEP ❸ While the noodles are cooking, blend the milk, cooked potato pieces, and seasoning packet in the blender until the mixture is smooth. Set aside.

STEP ❹ When the noodles are done, drain off the water and put the noodles back into the pan. Pour the blender mixture over the noodles and heat the soup over medium heat until hot. When hot, pour into a bowl and sprinkle with the green onions. Enjoy.

▨ Microwave Directions

STEP ❶ Put the potato pieces in a microwave safe bowl and microwave approximately 3-4 minutes or until you can pierce them easily with a fork.

STEP ❷ Put the noodles and water in a microwave safe bowl. Microwave for 3-4 minutes or until they are done to your liking.

STEP ❸ While the noodles are cooking, blend the milk, cooked potato pieces, and seasoning packet in the blender until the mixture is smooth. Set aside.

STEP ❹ When the noodles are done, drain off the water and put the noodles back into the microwave safe bowl. Pour the blender mixture over the noodles and microwave for approximately one minute or until hot. When hot, sprinkle the green onions on top and enjoy.

Creamy Spinach Soup

1	chicken Ramen noodle package (crunch up while in package)
2	cups water
1	cup cold milk
1	large handful of spinach leaves
2	tablespoons Parmesan cheese
1	tablespoon all-purpose flour
¼	teaspoon garlic powder

Step ❶ This step can be done on the stovetop or in the microwave.

In a small pan, bring the water to a boil. Add the noodles and cook them to your liking.

Put the noodles and water in a microwave safe bowl. Microwave for 3-4 minutes or until they are done to your liking.

Step ❷ When the noodles are done, drain off the water and put the noodles into a bowl.

Step ❸ While the noodles are cooking, in a separate bowl stir the flour, seasoning packet, and garlic powder into the milk until smooth and there are no lumps.

Step ❹ Pour the milk mixture into the pan over medium heat. While the sauce is heating, tear or chop the spinach leaves and stir them into the sauce until they wilt or shrink down in size and the soup has thickened (the longer you cook it the thicker it will get, so cook it to your choice of consistency).

Step ❺ When the spinach leaves have wilted and the sauce is hot, stir in the Parmesan cheese.

Step ❻ Add the noodles to the pan and mix well.

Pour into a bowl and enjoy.

Egg Drop Soup

1   Ramen noodle package (any flavor)
     (crunch up while in package)

4   cups water

1   egg

1   green onion, chopped

STEP ❶ This step can be done on the stovetop or
       in the microwave.

In a small pan, bring 2 cups of water to a
boil. Add the noodles and cook them to
your liking.

Put the noodles and 2 cups of the water
in a microwave safe bowl. Microwave for
3-4 minutes or until they are done to your
liking.

STEP ❷ When the noodles are done, drain off the
       water and put the noodles into a serving
       bowl.

STEP ❸ Put the remaining 2 cups of water into a
       small pan. If you used a pan to cook the
       noodles, you can reuse that pan. Bring the
       water to a boil.

STEP ❹ While the water is heating up, scramble
       the egg in a small bowl.

STEP ❺ When the water is boiling, stir the seasoning packet into the water.

STEP ❻ Slowly stir the broth from the outer edge of the pan while slowly pouring the scrambled egg into the broth in a thin stream. Stir slowly until all the egg has been added and cooked, which should take less than a minute.

STEP ❼ When the egg is cooked, pour the broth over the noodles. Sprinkle the green onions on top and enjoy.

Crispy Fried Ramen

1   Ramen noodle package (any flavor)
(crunch up while in package)

2   cups water

1   tablespoon butter

1   tablespoon vegetable cooking oil

STEP ❶ This step can be done on the stovetop or in the microwave.

In a small pan, bring the water to a boil. Add the noodles and cook them to your liking.

Put the noodles and water in a microwave safe bowl. Microwave for 3-4 minutes or until they are done to your liking.

STEP ❷ Place the butter and oil in a skillet over medium heat.

STEP ❸ When the noodles are done, drain off the water and put the noodles into the hot skillet. Sprinkle on the seasoning packet and stir into the noodles.

STEP ❹ Spread the noodles out evenly to cover the bottom of the pan. Let the noodles fry until one side is crispy. Flip and cook the other side.

STEP ❺ When both sides are crispy, remove to a plate and enjoy.

Quick Dessert

Can be cooked entirely on stovetop or in microwave

1	Ramen noodle package (crunch up while in package)
	(This recipe will not use the seasoning packet)
2	cups water
1	banana, peeled and sliced
1	tablespoon butter
1 ½	teaspoon sugar
¼	teaspoon cinnamon

STEP ❶ This step can be done on the stovetop or in the microwave.

Bring the water to a boil in a small pan. Add the noodles and cook them to your liking.

Put the noodles and water in a microwave safe bowl. Microwave for 3-4 minutes or until the noodles are done to your liking.

STEP ❷ When the noodles are done, drain off the water and put them into a bowl.

STEP ❸ Add the butter, sugar, and cinnamon to the noodles and toss to blend until all butter is melted and mixed in.

STEP ❹ Toss in the banana slices and enjoy.

Can be cooked entirely on stovetop or in microwave

Lemon Chicken Noodles

1   chicken Ramen noodle package (crunch up while in package)

2   cups water

1   tablespoon or so of fresh or bottled lemon juice (amount based on preference)

1-2   tablespoons of fresh cilantro or parsley leaves

⅛   teaspoon black pepper or more to taste

STEP ❶ This step can be done on the stovetop or in the microwave.

In a small pan, bring the water to a boil. Add the noodles and seasoning packet and cook them to your liking.

Put the noodles, seasoning packet, and water in a microwave safe bowl. Microwave for 3-4 minutes or until done to your liking.

STEP ❷ When the noodles are done, drain the water off and put the noodles into a bowl.

STEP ❸ Toss the cilantro or parsley, pepper, and lemon juice to taste with the noodles. Enjoy.

Oriental Coleslaw

1   Ramen noodle package (crunch up while in package)

 (This recipe does not use the seasoning packet)

2   pressed cups pre-shredded bagged coleslaw mix (found in the produce section of the grocery store)

1   tablespoon toasted sesame oil (see note below)

2   tablespoons seasoned rice vinegar (see note below)

1   teaspoon soy sauce

½   teaspoon sugar

STEP ❶ In a medium size bowl toss the dry noodles with the coleslaw mix.

STEP ❷ In a separate bowl, mix the oil, vinegar, soy sauce, and sugar. Stir until the sugar is fully dissolved.

STEP ❸ Pour the sauce over the noodles and coleslaw mixture and toss well. Enjoy.

Note: The toasted sesame oil and seasoned rice vinegar can be found in the Asian section of the grocery store.

Noodles 'n Cheese

1   Ramen noodle package (crunch up while in package)

   (This recipe does not use the seasoning packet)

2   cups of water

3   tablespoons milk

½   teaspoon butter

2   slices of American cheese, torn into smaller pieces

   pinch of salt

 Stovetop directions

STEP ❶ In a small pan, bring the water to a boil. Add the noodles to the boiling water and cook them to your liking.

STEP ❷ When the noodles are done, drain off the water and put the noodles back into the pan. Reduce the heat to medium low.

STEP ❸ Add the milk and butter to the noodles and stir until the butter is melted.

STEP ❹ After the butter has melted, stir the pieces of cheese and salt into the noodles until the cheese is fully melted and the sauce is smooth. Pour into a bowl and enjoy.

⬚ Microwave Directions

STEP ❶ Put the noodles and water in a microwave safe bowl. Microwave for 3-4 minutes or until they are done to your liking. When the noodles are done, drain off the water and put the noodles back into the bowl.

STEP ❷ Stir the butter, milk, and the pieces of cheese into the noodles.

STEP ❸ Microwave for 15 seconds, stop and stir. Repeat for another 15 seconds. Remove from the microwave and stir until the cheese is fully melted and the sauce is smooth. Enjoy.

Oriental Peanut Soup

1	oriental Ramen noodle package (crunch up while in package)
2	cups water
1	green onion, chopped
1	small carrot, peeled
¾	teaspoon peanut butter, smooth

Stovetop directions

STEP ❶ In a small pan, bring the water to a boil.

STEP ❷ While the water is heating, use a vegetable peeler to slice thin strips of carrot into a bowl. Keep slicing until the carrot gets real small and it becomes difficult to peel any more off (these thin strips will cook super fast).

STEP ❸ When the water is boiling, add the carrot slices, noodles, and seasoning packet.

STEP ❹ When the noodles are close to being done, add the green onions and peanut butter. Stir until the peanut butter is fully dissolved.

STEP ❺ When the noodles are done, pour into a bowl and let cool slightly before eating as it will be very hot. Enjoy.

▦ Microwave Directions

STEP ❶ Use a vegetable peeler to slice thin strips of carrot into a bowl. Keep slicing until the carrot gets real small and it becomes difficult to peel any more off (these thin strips will cook super fast).

STEP ❷ In a microwave safe bowl, combine the noodles, water, carrot strips, and seasoning packet. Microwave for 3-4 minutes or until the noodles are done to your liking.

STEP ❸ When the noodles are done, stir in the green onions and peanut butter until the peanut butter is fully dissolved. Enjoy.

Pork 'n Beans 'n Noodles

(Makes an oversized serving)

1   pork Ramen noodle package (crunch up while in package)

1   cup water

1   can of pork and beans, any size will work

1-2 hot dogs, sliced

Stovetop directions

STEP ❶ Put the sliced hot dogs into a small pan with the water. Bring the water to a boil.

STEP ❷ When the water is boiling, add the crunched up noodles and seasoning packet and cook to your liking.

STEP ❸ When the noodles are done, stir in the can of pork and beans. Continue to cook until the soup is hot. Pour into a large bowl and enjoy.

Microwave Directions

STEP ❶ Put the water, noodles, hot dogs, and seasoning packet in a large microwave safe bowl. Stir well. Microwave for 3-4 minutes or until the noodles are done to your liking.

STEP ❷ Remove from the microwave and stir in the can of pork and beans. Microwave for 1 more minute or until the soup is hot. Enjoy.

Ramen Alfredo

1   chicken Ramen noodle package (crunch up while in package)

2   cups water

½   teaspoon all-purpose flour

¼   cup Parmesan cheese

½   cup milk or half and half

1 ½ teaspoon butter

¼   teaspoon garlic powder or 1 garlic clove, minced

STEP ❶ This step can be done on the stovetop or in the microwave.

In a small pan, bring the water to a boil. Add the noodles and seasoning packet and cook them to your liking.

Put the noodles, seasoning packet, and water in a microwave safe bowl and microwave for 3-4 minutes or until they are done to your liking.

STEP ❷ When the noodles are done, drain off the water and put the noodles in a bowl. Set aside.

STEP ❸ In a separate bowl, stir the flour into the milk or half and half until smooth and there are no lumps.

STEP ❹ Put a small pan over medium heat. Put the cheese, flour and milk or half and half mixture, garlic, and butter into the pan and stir until the cheese is melted.

STEP ❺ Pour the sauce over the noodles, toss to mix, and enjoy.

Ramen Chili

(Makes an oversized serving)

1	beef Ramen noodle package (crunch up while in package)
2	cups water
1	15-oz. can of chili (your preference of brand and type of chili)
1	slice of American cheese, torn into several pieces
	One handful of corn chips (optional)

Stovetop directions

STEP ❶ In a medium pan, bring the water to a boil. Add the noodles and cook them to your liking.

STEP ❷ After the noodles are done, drain off the water and put the noodles back into the pan over the heat.

STEP ❸ Add the can of chili and seasoning packet to the noodles in the pan. Mix well. When it is hot, add the cheese and stir until melted and mixed in.

STEP ❹ Pour it into a bowl and crumble the corn chips on top. Enjoy.

≈▦ Microwave Directions

STEP ❶ Put the noodles and water in a large microwave safe bowl. Microwave for 3-4 minutes or until they are done to your liking. When the noodles are done, drain off the water and put them back into the bowl.

STEP ❷ Pour the can of chili over the noodles and stir in the seasoning packet.

STEP ❸ Microwave for 1 minute to heat through. Stir the cheese into the noodles and microwave for 30 seconds more to melt the cheese.

STEP ❹ Remove from microwave and stir until the melted cheese is mixed in. Crumble the corn chips on top and enjoy.

Spaghetti Ramen

1   beef Ramen noodle package (crunch up while in package)

2   cups water

1   cup of your favorite spaghetti sauce (to make your own see recipe on next page)

2   teaspoons Parmesan cheese (optional)

Stovetop directions

STEP ❶ In a small pan, bring the water to a boil. Add the noodles and seasoning packet and cook them to your liking.

STEP ❷ When the noodles are done, drain off the water and return the noodles to the pan over medium low heat.

STEP ❸ Pour the sauce over the noodles and cook until hot.

STEP ❹ Pour into a bowl, sprinkle the Parmesan cheese on top, and enjoy.

Microwave Directions

STEP ❶ Put the water, noodles, and seasoning packet in a microwave safe bowl and microwave for 3-4 minutes or until they are done to your liking.

STEP ❷ When the noodles are done, drain off the water and return the noodles to the bowl.

STEP ❸ Pour the sauce over the noodles and return to the microwave for up to 1 minute or until the sauce is hot. Sprinkle the Parmesan cheese on top and enjoy.

To make your own sauce

1	teaspoon sugar
1	teaspoon oregano or Italian seasoning
½	teaspoon garlic powder
1	8-oz. can of tomato sauce

In a separate bowl mix all of the ingredients. Set aside.

Spicy Ranch

1   chicken Ramen noodle package (crunch up while in package)

2   cups water

1   tablespoon + 1 ½ teaspoons ranch salad dressing

Red Rooster Sriracha hot chili sauce (Amount based on preference)

1   small tomato, diced

salt to taste

1   bell pepper, diced (optional)

STEP ❶ This step can be done on the stovetop or in the microwave.

In a small pan, bring the water to a boil. Add the noodles and seasoning packet and cook them to your liking.

Put the noodles, seasoning packet, and water in a microwave safe bowl. Microwave for 3-4 minutes or until they are done to your liking.

STEP ❷ When the noodles are done, pour them into a strainer and drain off the water. Run cold water over the noodles until they are cold. Drain well.

STEP ❸ Put the noodles into a bowl. Add the ranch dressing, tomato, a pinch of salt, bell pepper, and the hot sauce to taste.

STEP ❹ Toss until mixed and enjoy.

Stir Fry Ramen

1   Ramen noodle package (crunch up while in package)

     (This recipe does not use the seasoning packet)

2   cups water

2   cups frozen stir fry vegetables

2   heaping tablespoons of your favorite sweet and sour or stir fry sauce

2   tablespoons peanut or vegetable oil

STEP ❶ Put the frozen vegetables in a strainer and rinse with hot water for about 30 seconds. Set aside to thaw and drain.

STEP ❷ This step can be done on the stovetop or in the microwave.

In a small pan bring the water to a boil. Add the noodles and cook them to your liking.

Put the noodles and water in a microwave safe bowl. Microwave for 3-4 minutes or until they are done to your liking.

STEP ❸ When the noodles are done, drain off the water and set the noodles aside.

Caution: In the next step, the oil may pop when you add the vegetables!!!

Step ❹ Place the oil in a skillet over medium heat. When the oil is hot, add the vegetables and toss. Cook until they are tender but not mushy.

Step ❺ When the vegetables are tender, add the noodles and the sweet and sour sauce.

Step ❻ Toss the mixture until the sauce is mixed in evenly. Pour onto a plate and enjoy.

Tortilla Soup

1   chicken Ramen noodle package (crunch up while in package)

2   cups water

1   cup frozen mixed vegetables

1   teaspoon of a taco seasoning packet

1   slice of American cheese, torn into smaller pieces

1   handful of corn chips, crushed

Stovetop directions

STEP ❶ Put the frozen vegetables and the water into a small pan. Bring the water to a boil.

STEP ❷ When the water is boiling, add the noodles, taco seasoning, and seasoning packet. Cook them to your liking.

STEP ❸ After the noodles are done, reduce the heat to medium low and add the cheese.

STEP ❹ Stir the noodles until the cheese is fully melted. Pour the soup into a bowl and top with the corn chips. Enjoy.

Microwave Directions

STEP ❶ Put the frozen vegetables, water, noodles, seasoning packet, and taco seasoning in a microwave safe bowl. Microwave for 5 minutes or until the noodles are done to your liking.

STEP ❷ Add the cheese and stir until it is completely melted. Top with the corn chips. Enjoy.

Tuna Ramen Casserole

(Makes an oversized serving)

1   chicken Ramen noodle package (crunch up while in package)

1   cup water

1   cup cold milk

1   cup frozen mixed vegetables

1 ½   tablespoons all-purpose flour (you can use only 1 Tablespoon if you want it thinner)

1   6-oz. can tuna, drained

2   teaspoons butter

½   teaspoon dill seed

STEP ❶ In a small pan, add the water, dill seed, vegetables, and seasoning packet and bring to a boil. When the water is boiling, add the noodles. Cook until the noodles are done to your liking.

STEP ❷ While the noodles are cooking, in a separate bowl stir the flour into the milk until smooth and there are no lumps.

STEP ❸ When the noodles are done, add the milk and flour mixture, butter, and tuna to the pan. Stir it continually over the heat until the soup is hot. (The longer you cook it, the thicker it will get, so stop at your choice of consistency. It will also thicken more as it cools.)

STEP ❹ When the soup is at your choice of consistency, pour into a bowl. Enjoy.

About the Authors

Kimberly Prescott, author of *When Your Baby's on a Budget*, is in the kitchen this time providing money-saving ideas with Ramen. She has always loved cooking, so when her son Skyler, who is a college student, presented her with the concept of making instant Ramen noodles better, it was right up her alley. Skyler wanted recipes that embody the simplicity, affordability, and great taste of instant Ramen.

Together, with Skyler's creativity and Kimberly's cooking expertise, they have made the Ramen experience an even more delicious indulgence.

For more information or to see
some of these recipes made visit:
thelowbudgetwonder.com